Flood, Fire & Drought

Flood, Fire & Drought

Edited by
Suzanne Edgar, Kathy Kituai,
Sandra Renew & Hazel Hall

Flood, Fire & Famine
ISBN 978 1 74027 929 1
Copyright © poems individual poets 2015
Views expressed are those of the contributing poets
and not necessarily of the editors.

First published 2015 by
Ginninderra Press
PO Box 3461 Port Adelaide SA 5015
www.ginninderrapress.com.au

Contents

Foreword		**7**
Preface		**9**
Reflections		**11**
Bonfire	Moya Pacey	13
The Old Fireplace	Denise Burton	14
Before Copenhagen	Hazel Hall	15
Set the Bonfire	Gregory Piko	16
Home Editing	Rod Usher	17
Two Rivers	Suzanne Edgar	19
Flood		**21**
Too Much	Jennie Fraine	23
Flood	Fiona McIlroy	24
Shadow	Brenda Saunders	25
New York Sonnet	Brenda Saunders	26
still swirling through my mind	Kathy Kituai	27
Fire		**29**
It's Spring – the Ash Tree Dances	John Stokes	31
A Fire Has No Conscience	Peter Kunz	32
fire haiku	PS Cottier	33
Bushfire Battlefield	Joe Massingham	34
Four Fires	Paul Williamson	35
Firestorm	Helga Jermy	36
Famine		**37**
Famine Inside	Mira Walker	39
Cull	Hazel Hall	40
hungry for pippies and sticky rice	Kathy Kituai	42
Rabbit-oh	Adrienne White	43
Famine	John Collard	44
Three days from hunger	Sandra Renew	45
Promise	Bob Morrow	46

Aftermath   47
Family Tree	Suzanne Edgar	49
The Start of Days	Paul Williamson	50
Apologies	Victoria McGrath	51
Burning Off	Lizz Murphy	52
Barely a Torso	Kathryn Yuen	53
Sell and Regret, But Sell	Robyn Sykes	54
Triangle Fire	Cassandra Atherton	55
Flood, Fire and Drought	Sandra Renew	56

Renaissance   57
Drought	John Collard	59
Heat wave	Lizz Murphy	60
After the Drought	Jennie Fraine	61

The Music Of Climate   63
Playing With Fire	Moya Pacey	65
Bloodforms: Groundfire	John Stokes	67
Hunter River Valley	June Foster	68
Conflagration	Monica Carroll	69
Ancient and Proud	Maree Teychenné	71
Prometheus: Poem of Fire (Op. 60)	Victoria McGrath	73
Fire Song	Henry Ashley-Brown	74

Contributors   75

Foreword

The School of Music (SOM) Poets is an ekphrastic group. Its goal is to explore relationships between verse, music and other art forms and express these through poetry and song lyrics. To that end, our poets explore a wide range of rich artistic experiences. SOM Poets has its genesis in the Café Poets program sponsored by Australian Poetry. Its co-sponsor is Biginelli Espresso, School of Music, Australian National University (ANU). We thank our sponsors for making this anthology possible, and also Professor Peter Tregear, Head of the SOM ANU, for his enthusiastic support.

Based on its threefold title theme, *Flood, Fire & Drought* brings together works by Australian poets and songwriters in an anthology exploring both the hardships of nature and the resilience of those facing and managing them. The final section in the anthology is devoted to music-related poetry, including song lyrics.

We are deeply grateful to all who submitted poems, with special thanks to the editorial team consisting of Suzanne Edgar, Kathy Kituai and Sandra Renew. Without their patient advice and support, this anthology could not have been compiled. We also thank Kathy Kituai for her layout ideas and advice. Although most of the poems were written without political intent, at this critical time in the world's history, we asked Richard Denniss, Executive Director of The Australia Institute, to provide a context for our collection. We thank him for his time and effort in doing so and hope that these poetic stories will strike a chord with the wider public.

Finally, I wish to thank my partner Christopher Dorman for his unfailing technical assistance during the compiling of this anthology.

Hazel Hall
Australian Poetry Café Poet in Residence
Facilitator of School of Music Poets
Biginelli Espresso, School of Music, Australian National University

Preface

When an economist is asked to write a preface for a book of poetry, it's obvious that we do indeed live in interesting times.

Climate change has been described as many things: a great moral challenge, a wicked problem, the biggest economic threat we have ever faced, a hoax. Like climate change itself, describing it is unavoidable.

Words shape our perception of the things they describe. Words make us feel emotions ranging from joy to rage. And more than any other words, poetry seeks to shape the way we feel.

Much of the debate about climate change rightly revolves around science. The science tells us that some gases trap heat more effectively than others. The science tells us that the more heat-trapping gases we put into the atmosphere, the warmer it will get. And the scientists tell us that as the seas and atmosphere warm, the climate will change, the seas will rise and our lives will change. Just as scientists can't tell us where on our body too much sun will cause skin cancer, climate scientists can't tell us exactly what a warmer planet will mean for our town or our country.

But while science can tell us much about what is happening, it is up to us as individuals to decide how we feel about what is happening. For some people, the uncertainty about exactly how climate change will affect their lives is a reason to ignore the issue altogether. For others, the uncertainty drives them to dedicate their life to reducing emissions. And, for most people perhaps, the uncertainty provides yet another source of anxiety that they don't know what to do about.

Scientists invented nuclear weapons, but they play very little role in shaping how people feel about nuclear war. Scientists invented antibiotics but they play very little role in deciding who should receive them. And scientists have invented alternative energy sources to the fossil fuels that cause so much of our climate change, but they play very little role in deciding how rapidly to deploy them.

While science can hold a magnifying glass over the world, poetry can hold a magnifying glass over our deepest emotions. If we are to tackle climate change, we must not just understand the world, but understand ourselves, and it is to that end that this volume is directed.

The poems that follow take us from the deeply personal impact of climate change on a woman forced to sell the family farm to the process of negotiations of global agreements. They take us on a journey across the landscape of flood, fire and drought.

Sunlight is the best disinfectant. Healthy debate and a healthy planet require us to throw open the windows and shed light on the problems we face, and our feelings about those problems. Thanks to the artists who made this volume possible, I hope that we can all better understand not just the world we live in, but our own responses to it.

Dr Richard Denniss
Executive Director, The Australia Institute

Reflections

I search through darker water
for a lost watercolour world

– Suzanne Edgar, 'Two Rivers'

Bonfire

In Ireland they burn the Pope.
In England it's Guy Fawkes
but nothing that is live –
no men in wicker baskets
no sacks of hissing serpents,
white cockerels or live cats,
foxes or squirrels –
suffers in my fire.

I feed mine with old shoes,
a chopped-up piano,
fence posts and orange boxes.
Anything I can loot.
Crackle and rush
My fire is built for play.
Jump over the fire
Warm my bones.

Moya Pacey

The Old Fireplace

Running through the house
naked and wet
from the nightly bath,
towel-wrapped
I flop in front
of the log fire.

Flames are flicking
logs into a
cheerful glow,
warmth drying
my body.

I am rubbed dry
by my mother
and snuggle
into special
winter pyjamas.

In reflection
layers of memory shine,
warmth
love
belonging
cradle me still
from the old fireplace.

Denise Burton

Before Copenhagen

that's worth a photo they said
just a man among friends
having a wine
on his 70th birthday
face wearing traces of intensity
eyes – shirt – jeans
more true blue than the sky
and the spotted dog trembling
with slobber want-to-jump-up gaze
plonked on his feet

you could take off
into that summer horizon
cloudy islets dotted over
half shaded by the Bunnings sail
trying to hold the Dorothea landscape
in its cruel beauty
for one moment
with the dry grass crackling
and brown hens cackling in their run –
unease in the slightest breeze –
tomorrow he'll check the fire truck
and wash the dishes
while his wife flies out
to Copenhagen

Hazel Hall

Set the Bonfire

Leathery heat from a northerly —
withered leaves, each one
dry as a drover's tongue
a nightmare of flame
towers like a tidal wave.

Of course, I've done all I can.
Closed the windows,
drained the pool and
set the bonfire, for that they say
should save the house.

Now, assured,
I await my fate,
to defend
face down amid a wash
of splintered timbers.

Gregory Piko

Home Editing

for Helen Garner

Daily bread gone verdigris,
volumes of your recorded life die:
'a bundle, a seethe, a swarm, a wisp,
and then those soft grey feathers'
you write with unflinching eye.
I picture you poker-wielding
in your Melbourne garden
– pages clinging to past –
and would love to have browsed,
secretly doused a year or two
mined the gold and dross
of unexpurgated diary you.

I recall your self-editing prowess
as in the big field, permit in pocket,
I burn nature's clunky ms:
chapters of wind-dropped wattle
cliché blackberries, less-is-more prunings
purple prose of the overwrought willow
amid shoot-outs, piercing sap cries,
florid tongue and grey billow.
At midnight it's rake and slake,
embers briefly answering those overhead.
Daylight brings an off-white page,
all the 'darlings' now dead.

Rod Usher

Two Rivers

Mourning, here, by Molongolo,
its thistled banks and dry swamps,
I search through darker water
for a lost watercolour world.

There was a place where all birds sang
and only jersey cows intruded;
a willowy green space
framed by the tallest gums.

We'd walk a winding path
past the small stone house,
hollyhocks, roses, a grassy
slope down to the last gate.

Unlatch and run to the river bank
with the red wooden dinghy.
It was a place, always summer,
where the parents never quarrelled,

where my dad made time
to teach me how to row
in narrow tricky Onkaparinga.
Once launched on the water,

we reached for blackberries,
fat and black, dripping juice.
Yabbies nibbled our bait
that swayed in the flow.

And this translucent green
gave every pebble colour,
gave ferns their freckled shade…
We always stayed till the light had gone.

Suzanne Edgar

Flood

a man
locked in his car
still swirling through my mind

– Kathy Kituai, 'still swirling through my mind'

Too Much

Whenever the rains tumble down, now
it seems shocking that the sky can gush
so liberally. We accepted desiccation
as the norm. How are we to take
for granted every deluge, each storm?

The earth, couch grass, nameless weeds
as well as callistemon, caesia, grevillea
take advantage, draw while the well
is bottomless, and store, grow taller.
I capture these wild waters, ignore them.

What can you do, after saving every drop
for years? The garden doesn't need our
benevolence. Hoarse laughter, flashing eyes
from the sky: more rain and more, as if
the clouds themselves are desperate to be dry.

Jennie Fraine

Flood

a flood of tears
a flurry of ideas
a flock of worries
a fresco of dreams
a float
of hopeful refugees

Fiona McIlroy

Shadow

Brought in on a rip he's trapped
in the channel just off the beach
A sandbar blocks his way

No room to turn or manoeuvre
he waits for change, daylight –
a high tide to lift him out to sea

A fisherman on the empty beach
watches the shadow cruising
Waves his arms, cries out

Running in water, I grasp at air
drag the weight of sand, turn
to see a grey nurse take the swell

Fear drifting out from the shore

Brenda Saunders

New York sonnet

She's a city ringed with water
a shoreline patched with wharves.
Streets criss-cross the avenues
running to the sea. Block by block
the buildings blur the middle distance
crowd grey skies downtown. A trumpet
catches a riff, his notes lifting like steam
from a sidewalk in the Village.
The Big Apple's ready for the bite
the zing and sting of days lived
at the sharp edge of new. People
ride the A train, keep ahead of time.
Movers with a taste for change know
which way is up, the word 'to go'.

Brenda Saunders

still swirling through my mind
tanka

1

in the rubble
after losing everything
a pink hat
the one her mother made
last week for charity

always the first
to man the fire hose
the last
in his troupe to be told
the home he built had gone

only a few
eucalypts now smouldering
in the wake
satin-soft first shoots
sprouting in blackened bark

2

road signs
above storm water
pointing
straight ahead
into darkness

twelve confirmed dead
fifty-six still missing
a man
locked in his car
still swirling through my mind

mud removed
the house hosed clean
he hammers
firmly into place
a FOR SALE sign

3

how to imagine
losing your home to flood
fire and cyclone?
broom mid-air, I hesitate
to sweep your web from the eaves

Kathy Kituai

Fire

firies make their way home,
mist a twisted string through trees
powerless wires and shock

– Helga Jermy, 'Firestorm'

It's Spring – the Ash Tree Dances

It's spring – the ash tree dances
Imagine you can see the women burning
Imagine the Kalashnikovs, their singing
Into the roaring of those eyes.

Feel, now, the crack of the skull-grin
Feel the brown woman starving
See her death under lights, the better
To make the NEWS, to make the NEWS.

The sky is a mirror held by strangers
Talking in tongues; see, how she falls
How she falls; it makes a picture
Her men are crowding round, crowding round.

See her men are crowding round; that boned one
Staring earthward, she is staring earthward
She is drawing her little cloth around her groin
She is dancing in the shimmering veil.

John Stokes

A Fire Has No Conscience

Beware
A fire has no conscience
He burns at will
A lit match tossed to the ground
Or lightning strike will create the monster
Whose appetite will not be quenched
By ordinary means

If you were to ask him to leave
This psychopath
Etched in orange
Will leap at you in rage
His roiling parting gift
Will be
Only and always
Charred ashes

Peter Kunz

fire haiku

ash tales flutter
read the passing lives
darkening snow

*

silhouettes cut into red –
leaping through flames
a panic of kangaroos

*

delicate cup shell
amongst her house's ruins
cool willow pattern

PS Cottier

Bushfire Battlefield

At first a haze on the horizon
as if some stockman
were driving a mob of cattle home.

The rumbling thunder of guns,
army in the sky,
the sappers tunnel through clouds
in their sun-coloured disguise.

The echoing hooves of
Hell's cavalry, with
molten gold breastplates shining,
scarlet clouds of dust.

Leaping and slashing,
flickering swords
routing their path,
leaving scorched earth,
rivers full of heaven's blood.

Distorted shapes and residents,
blackened skeletons
along the skyline,

Acrid smoke
is the emptiness left of life.

Joe Massingham

Four Fires

So dry, rain doesn't find the ground.
Heavy winds blow then fade.
Fire fighters hold blazes.
Temperatures stay under forecast highs.
Sensing that danger has passed,
calm emerges from some hiding place.
People shop and drive back for their homes.

Volunteers stand down;
leave for home bases.
Fatigue dogged five smoke-haunted weeks.
Now desire is strong to reach
life's routines, professions, schools;
settled months for recharge.
Four fires smoulder in nearby forests.

Paul Williamson

Firestorm

Earth heat fries ash beneath a cinder sky,
sheets of buckled tin sculptures to loss.
Timid birds are Icarus – the skin
of cat paws smoulder in the rubble with books
and the debris of living.

In paddocks exhausted hides lie tanned.
In shelters exhausted lives lie stunned.

Firies make their way home.
Mist a twisted string through trees,
powerless wires and shock.

Helga Jermy

Famine

Back at the gate
he turns on the tap beside the cattle trough,
watches water seep
between a score of plants,
his face hard as the light.

– Bob Morrow, 'Promise'

Famine Inside

Suddenly,
your bones are poking through your skin.
At whom?
'Whaddareyou staring at?'
I don't know.

There are thick
jade bows
in cloth casing
on your bather's hips, thin
bones shrouded
with pallid skin,
hunched away from me;

There are ribs
barring hands
a last protection
for your seething lungs.

Later I seek talk:
no word is given,
a phrase remains
starving for attention
which seems incomplete…

Watching through your longest year,
as flesh slowly returns,
I wait for you.

Mira Walker

Cull

Can't let them starve. It's clean, humane, best practice. They're buried with no mess.

Sixteen hundred of them. Easy to catch off the hop. In that frozen moment, poised – silhouetted like paper cuts.

A single shot is all it takes. Shine the flash. Light to eye – eye to light – and fire. One goes down. The others scatter. You get more as they go. For a moment, you might see shadows rising from the carcasses – drifting for a few minutes – then fading into the haze of the night. Your nerves are wire.

sometimes
a leap in faith…
she releases
two orphans raised
in supermarket bags

Hazel Hall

hungry for pippies and sticky rice

I can't imagine what it must be like
to wait for the next quake or tsunami, the next
falling down of faith.

In Christchurch last week
aftershocks dismantled roofs,
newly fitted window panes

and gnawed what was left
of Aufi's confidence
night after dream-deprived night.

Was he hungry for twilight
where crickets practise riffs, and frogs
baritone blissful hours into dawn?

What must it be like wondering
if you should shelter in a doorway
shouldering the weight of your family home

filled with memories of your mother sautéing pippies,
telephone wires swaying overhead
like power-struck politicians?

A breeze is chatting up
last month's autumn leaves
fan-tan-going down my driveway.

I can't imagine governments
or mining corporations
celebrating such seasonal bliss.

In Fukushima
they've found strontium in groundwater
near No. 1 nuclear power station

after measuring radiation levels
117 times above safety standards
at the intake outlet of No. 2 reactor

on 67 occasions.
Is Mariko wondering whether paddy fields
in which Yuki San sowed rice

sticky enough to roll just so
to place into your mouth
are contaminated, or what it will be like
to go hungry?

Kathy Kituai

Rabbit-oh

When I was young, of no renown,
I bought rabbits by the one, two, three.
I'd buy them from the man in town,
who'd cry *rabbit-oh, rabbit-oh* to me.
Then I'd take them back home.
And, on my way, pockets too light for grog,
the men passing would moan,
You can't eat that – it's fit for a dog.
But my mother, she'd say,
Is that it, where's the rest?
Is that all for us today?
And she'd say I let that old pest
get the better of me.
She'd talk about Scullin and Lang's stand,
and how it'd be better next year, in 1933.
How we'd be better off on the land,
or worse by half – she didn't know.
But she wanted us not to owe
and me to be the one to crow,
rabbit-oh, rabbit-oh.

Adrienne White

Famine

Demons dreadlock a Drysdale landscape;
bleached gums
quaver before tormenting winds,
Golgotha skulls decorate barren soil.

A housewife fortressed between stone walls
pins winding sheets to thorn trees.
Hounds strain at leashes
eager for pickings.

John Collard

Three Days From Hunger

If the fuel does not
go into the trucks,
and planes and boats,
to bring us food
in our mega cities,
we are three days from hunger.

This thin veneer
of global civilisation
depends on fossil fuel
and a lack of care
and love
for the generations now and to come.

The rightfully unforgiving planet
will punish us,
when the dry soil becomes dust
and the hot winds blow grit,
and the trucks do not come.

Then we will know
that the first world, heating up,
will become the third world,
hot, hungry, homeless,
and moving south.

Sandra Renew

Promise

His best paddock,
wheat still green, resisting.
This bit over to the fence
should have given us two thousand bags.
We'll get two hundred if we're lucky,
not even next year's seed.

He plucks an ear,
chews the stem,
tastes its sweet juice,
counts husks plump with promise,
splits one with a blackened fingernail,
reveals pale speck of grain in silken caul,
one dry week from miscarriage.
Between the rows, the dark-damp
soil of sowing time has set,
crazed with cracks which swallow hope.

This could still be a good crop.
If we got fifty points tonight,
it could last another week,
and if we had four inches follow-up…
Words echo off a sky brittle as blue porcelain.
September sun slides down.
Cool breeze brings no consolation.

Back at the gate,
he fills the cattle trough,
watches water seep
between a score of plants,
his face hard as the light.

Bob Morrow

Aftermath

…we recognise ourselves
in the smallest elements of our catastrophes…
– Sandra Renew, 'Flood, Fire and Drought'

Family Tree

In the scarlet storm of a fire
a towering gum tree sank
onto weakened haunches.
The belly was ripped apart

leaving a great black hole,
crown and every branch
vanished into ash:
a headless torso remains.

Close against the gum
is one whose lower limbs
are wrapped around the source
like a parent's clinging child.

This other, younger, tree
has grown up tall and strong.
Its smooth and speckled branches
are clothed in lucent green

that forms a canopy,
a new and noisy world
alive with breeding birds
all unaware of the past.

Suzanne Edgar

The Start of Days

Our home is on a tree-lined slope;
my wife, out of contact.
She might come.
Worried, we wait
before we leave for Nana's.

The phone rings.
Bundle children into the car.
Fires burn near the road.
Do you see smoke? Yes.
Do you see flames? No.

Still time to be safe.
Crews work through the night
to stop and save.
By dawn the heat and wind are gone.
Cars on the road to home

don't seem panicked.
Our house still stands
covered in soot.
Smoke ribbons rise from tree stumps.
Smell of fire.

Time to clean, reclaim our lives
until the next peak fire time.
The start of days.

Paul Williamson

Apologies

Last night, a suntanned girl on the national news
lamented: expect higher than average
rainfall this summer, she said.
Sorry, so sorry.

Today I look out over our half-cooked crop, watch
the parrots pick at wizened weeds, listen
to the shrunken stalks rattling
in an overheated breeze,

and wonder what they'll all be eating this season.
Sorry, so sorry.

Victoria McGrath

Burning Off

Brassy wheat stubble blackening earth summer-dried threads
At home I clean out old coals screw up sheets of newsprint
remember how paper smells when it burns lay red eucalypt
twigs one over the other collect sawn logs from the season's first
delivery Loose tin rustles to the right what animal Slow turn
of the head slow old echidna soot-dark quills cream scorch-
brown tips It seeks shelter behind a scrap of iron a timber beam
draws into its body round as a football thorny The last sighting
of an echidna on our patch was after one of life's close shaves
Clambering out of the car we watched as it spun down into
hardened ground inching like a post-hole digger the drought-fine
dust ashen on its back Echidna was our totem for a while

Lizz Murphy

Barely a Torso

After the Belvedere Torso: Athens, first century BC, sculptor unknown

My homeland has turned into a furnace,
Set me on fire,
Burning away my limbs and head.
I can't run,
I can't see,
I only feel pain,
Fire, you have burned a hole in my heart.

My homeland has turned into a flood,
Tried to drown me,
Washing away my limbs and head.
I can't breathe,
I can't float,
I only go under,
Flood, you destroy faster than water torture.

My homeland has turned into a desert,
Leaving me starving,
Eating away my limbs and head.
I can't move,
I can't sleep,
I only subsist,
Famine, you leave no fuel to continue.
I am barely a torso.

Kathryn Yuen

Sell and Regret, But Sell

An old cocky's advice:

                    'Kim, a farm's like two dice,
you can roll and lose twice, that's all.
On a farm with a debt, you must never forget:
you should sell and regret – but sell.
When the wool price drops down and a permanent frown
creases cheeks like a town-scuffed shawl,
when the rain's overdue, then your choices are few:
feed the sheep till it's through – or sell.

'You can lighten off first before prices are worst;
to buy grain is to thirst for pain.
If the money's so tight that your sleep's wrecked all night,
though it hurts, you'll be right – to sell.
When the barley won't grow, stony rivers won't flow
and dry knees crackle low for rain;
before fuel bills fall due, city brothers blame you
and the grasses turn blue – please sell.

'As resilience bleeds, your accounts run to weeds.
Hear your child when he pleads, or wilt.
There's a life past the gate but don't leave it too late –
stand tall and stand straight – and sell.
My girl: drought's not a test, folk and paddocks need rest;
count your blessings is best, no guilt.
It's the end of my game; I've no blame and no shame.
When the trigger points came – I sold.'

Robyn Sykes

Triangle Fire

There is a photo
by an unknown photographer
that haunts me. It's the image
of a twisted ladder
that was once part of the fire escape
on the Asch building in New York.
It could almost be part of a spiral staircase
leading somewhere,
except that it is actually the remnants
of a collapsed fire escape
on which many, in 1911,
took their last step.

Cassandra Atherton

Flood, Fire and Drought

In our darkest, lowest moments,
our dread of the catastrophe of fire and flood and famine
gives us nightmares.
But, in reality, it's the small things,
a burning match,
a trickling tear drop,
the breakfast missed,
that shift us
from our even keel and mundane passage,
to being alive at the centre of our life.

As the arsonist, who flicks the match
that flares into conflagration,
as the boatman, whose concentration on the tiller
lapses momentarily while he wipes his tearing eyes
in the freezing gale force winds,
as the black marketeer who bargains with bags of rice
and tins of molasses under a truck's tarpaulin…
as these small players, we recognise ourselves
in the smallest elements of our catastrophes,
and, as these small players, despite ourselves,
we strive to leave a footprint, imprint, fingerprint,
feather light, as indiscernible as possible,
in the world's catastrophes.

Sandra Renew

Renaissance

Water sits in the bird baths, squinting
at springtime's pretty sun and she sits
on the patio, drinking in the blessed greens…

– Jennie Fraine, 'After the Drought'

Drought

Amidst the remnants of drought;
the dry brown hills,
the parched lake,
gray grasses bend before winter winds.
Yet wattles dare to strut their colours:
Jezebels at a barren harvest.

They thrust bosoms of blazing gold,
skirts of burnished green,
promise of fertility.
Spinster gums shake grizzled heads,
point barren hands in disbelief
at youthful foolishness.

Kangaroos twitch nervously in paddocks
for farmers grow trigger happy in drought years,
eager to protect scant pastures,
leaving streaked carcasses for carrion crows.

Yet still the wattles dance
to siren springtime breezes
when almond blossoms perfume air
and newborn lambs send trumpet calls.

John Collard

Heatwave

We gave them water and they sang their deep throat song

Lizz Murphy

After the Drought

This year's Euphorbia and Ecchia
have grown up, produced progeny.
The wattle no longer falls in strong winds

but flutters like a head of hair across
the new sand path. She relocates
a metal flamingo after pruning

the peppercorn tree; now there is
a pair. Even the loquat tree is proudly
parental, with two sprigs of hard golden fruit.

Wild oats have come and gone, rocket
and two-year-old silverbeet are as tall as she;
no need to bend for coriander either.

Water sits in the bird baths, squinting
at springtime's pretty sun and she sits
on the patio, drinking in the blessed greens

the rose perfumes, the immodesty
of bottle brushes, and wonders what to do
with all the buckets and bins of saved water.

Jennie Fraine

The Music of Climate

and we must search among the ticking stricken
metronome of black tree trunks...

– Henry Ashley-Brown, 'Firesong'

Playing With Fire

Lignum blaze smoke and smoulder
Steady flame against my shoulder

Whisper in my ardent ear
Fervent words I yearn to hear

Agni agni essence of fission
Agni agni pure ignition

Salamander Phoenix crackle frizzle
Salamander Loki cackle sizzle

'Rowling in the fiery Gulf'
Brand-Stifter rises – Ashen Wolf

Rearing mearing gnashing teeth
Heaving weaving a funeral wreath

Ignis flamma incendium
Conflagration has begun

Moya Pacey

Bloodforms: Groundfire

after *Sun Music*, in memory of Peter Sculthorpe

Burnt and shaved by slime
done fire dreaming
redhead comes eels and redeyed freckles girled
leathering along the shire-shivered, lone-eyed
lone-breasted hill. Night bound
thigh deep, travelling fast, the floozies scrubforest in
cloak and dagger dawn, skyfell
lost rips in smothered gullykiss, feathering

dieward, red in the drygrass

ground boned, haphazards

dry cock crowed
rustles, hapless, creeks of no-tree
Limbo or Shinto – all the same to the twist/
hiss of the limbless ones
who come to suck at stones and swallow fire.

These ghosts these
               Sisters
                            singe the eyeballs as nuns
beat & scatter hope; a blunt shriek
& runting bruise – groundflesh
traitoring taunting, under the groundswell, under
marsh burned, moistening pain
coal hunched, steam-heaved
hard known, veil ridged
still-remembered cries
thud walled behind the cliff face –
  bloodforms:

Imagined ground.
Love remembered water.

John Stokes

Hunter River Valley

From the high Mount Royal Ranges waters trickle down
to form the Hunter River near Murrurundi town.
Over time the people have experienced, no doubt
fire and flood and famine; disaster from the drought.

Nearby see Mount Wingen smouldering night and day;
a coal seam has been burning centuries away.
Over time those living there have experienced, no doubt
times of fierce fire; disaster from the drought.

On the central coast of New South Wales the Hunter meets the sea
carving out a flood plain valley that is steeped in history.
Over time those dwelling there have experienced, no doubt
flood and fire and famine; disaster from the drought.

Maitland floods bring life loss, rich soil swept out to sea;
the Hunter's witnessed hard times in its biography.
Those who have resided there have experienced, no doubt
hardship from the rains – from famine, fire and drought.

But the meandering river has brought wealth to those who toil;
graziers, miners, farmers who cultivate the soil.
All those who have settled there brought close, without a doubt
from unforeseen disaster: flood, fire, famine and drought.

June Foster

Conflagration

Walls turn fire
Hot pillow   Flip   Hot
No shirt to tear for air
Bed sheets tuck gullies

Hot pillow   Flip   Hot
Restless skin in midnight sheen
Bed sheets tuck gullies
Burning furnace, tongue-numb torment

Restless skin in midnight sheen
No shirt to tear for air
Burning furnace, tongue-numb torment
Walls turn fire

Monica Carroll

Ancient and Proud

Ancient and proud, horizons unbending,
she commands our attention,
this land without end.

And her mystery just deepens
as her history unfolds –
dangerous and charming
is the green and the gold.

Her fiery skies in the dead red desert,
raging storms that come from the sea,
her dusty-dry plains just after the rains
are all a great mystery,
great mystery to me.

You could go mad in her sun and bitter rain
and many's the man died cursing her name.

No one can tame her, nobody will,
for her charms can turn quickly
to heartbreak and pain.

Her fiery skies in the dead red desert,
raging storms that come from the sea,
her dusty-dry plains just after the rains
are all a great mystery,
great mystery to me.

*

So why is she calling, this spirit unending?
What is she saying?
What is she saying?

Why is she calling, this spirit unending?
It's all a great mystery,
all a great mystery to me.

So why is she calling?
What is she saying to me, to me?

Maree Teychenné
Music: Steven Capaldo

Prometheus: Poem of Fire (Op. 60)

after Scriabin

It opens on an ominous note, all about Prometheus sneaking
fire back from Zeus, who had hidden it from humans in a
fit of pique (long story!). Scriabin built it on the mystic chord,
designed it to reveal what is beyond human comprehension,

to fill that which is empty, the everything and the nothing.

He wrote it to be played on a *Clavier à lumières*, or Chromola,
a 'colour organ' which hadn't even been invented when
he set the notes to paper. He assigned a colour to each key,
to prove that nature is alive, that every soul's integral to a
wider universe. And he believed that it would boost the mood.
The symphony sounds, at first, like the score from a fifties
film and you can imagine a villain slinking at the periphery,

scoping out possibilities, gathering the fortitude to make
his stand, and you just know that this won't end well.

Then the piccolos pipe in and you can feel the flaunt of fire,
the shooting pinnacles of pain as A, D#, C# and B are fused
in an unstable congress, a dissonant mix of green and steel

devised to increase tension, make you realise that there are things
at stake here. Scriabin favoured neither harmony nor melody.
His resonance of sound and colour is a bonfire meant to stroke

the skin, then smack it back into the dust, suck the essence and
release it without reason. The bolstered brass, timpanis and
drums, build to a crescendo and in the heat you can sense reality
offering up its cells, smell the welding of the live and unalive
as one. And then a choir, vocalising vowels, a mass of human
howling before the climax of the piece. He ends it on F#, a triad

of bright blue to flood a squalid sky: the resolution of a lightning
flash, a sunny day, and you return to find the random remains of
what the fire didn't want: a chipped china teapot lid, a garden
gnome, an old tin of pre-decimal coins, your mother's left leg.

Victoria McGrath

Fire Song

Bushfire has peeled away our land's features,
left nothing intact, burnt all that we knew it by
and we must search among the ticking, stricken
metronome of black tree trunks, bereft of
birdsong, walking like dark smoke, unshaped,
as the soft brush of an owl's wing to quiz them;
singed sepia now our dreams without words.
The paper moon is not exempt from mourning
when the sullen smell of burnt flesh arrives at
dawn; it turns its back and scuttles from sight,
so strange a red dawn brightly moody and still,
filled with dreams of rain that do not assuage
the smouldering cinders and the bloated corpses
of the thundering white-eyed horses, riderless;
bolting silhouettes that leapt and cried so wildly
through hot, cracked tonguing of the flames.
We discover them, torn, beyond the barbed wire,
amongst old, long-forgotten engraved rocks,
the signs of those whose song lines went before,
who danced the names and hazards of this place,
whose mouths, we salt-filled, to lead us to water.
What should we sing about this Promised Land?

Henry Ashley-Brown

Contributors

Henry Ashley-Brown's publications include poetry and short stories. His poem, 'Falling Man at nine forty-one, Sept eleven', was winner of The University of Adelaide Bundey Prize in 2007. Several of his poems were adapted for performance on stage by the University of Adelaide players whilst he was undertaking his PhD in Creative Writing. He has, in addition, enjoyed design activities such as landscaping, jewellery and sculpture. In 2012 he was shortlisted for the Wakefield Press Unpublished Manuscript award and is currently working on a book of short stories.

Cassandra Atherton is a Senior Lecturer in Literary Studies and Creative Writing at Deakin University. She has published a book of literary criticism, *Flashing Eyes and Floating Hair* (2007), a book of poetry, *After Lolita* (2010), and a novel, *The Man Jar* (2010). She is currently working on a book, *Wise Guys*, about American public intellectuals.

Denise Burton: After growing up in Sydney and living in such diverse places as London and Billinudgel, I have spent almost two decades happily settled in Canberra. I write as a way of recording events in life that I feel warrant expression. The themes of my poetry reflect life experiences such as raising children, travelling, family, family history and living in the country. The poem in this anthology taps into my memories of childhood. Canberra's active poetry scene has given me the opportunity to get involved in writing groups and performances at festivals and functions in Canberra and the region.

Monica Carroll has been published in a variety of journals and anthologies such as the *Burley*, *Picaro Press Poetry*, *DecomP*, *Poetrix*, *Cordite*, *Block*, *Antipodean*, *Idiom* and *New Australasian Writing*. She has won many awards and performs regularly in Canberra. In addition to writing, Monica likes to mix concrete.

John Collard is an ACT poet and writer who has published both here and abroad. He won the Mindscapes Competition in 2011. John's first poetry collection, with an Irish theme, was *The Manic Clock* (2011). It was followed by *Sugar Loaf and Humming Birds* (with Hazel Hall) in 2013. When John isn't engaged in the 2014 Peace Project, which takes a great deal of his time and passion, he works on his cultural history *From County Clare to Axedale and Beyond*.

PS Cottier writes poetry and the occasional short story. She lives in Canberra, where she completed a PhD on Charles Dickens at the Australian National University. She blogs at pscottier.com. P.S. Cottier edited *The Stars Like Sand: Australian Speculative Poetry* (Interactive Publications, 2014), along with Tim Jones of New Zealand.

Suzanne Edgar is a Canberra poet. Her recent books are *Still Life* (Picaro Press) and *The Love Procession* (Ginninderra Press), both 2012.

June Foster was born in Singleton NSW in 1927 and has resided in Canberra since 1953. She enjoys reading, writing, storytelling and studying nature. June has won a number of competitions for her lyric poetry and is represented in various local anthologies including *Mondays at Tilley's* (1999), *Australian Spirit* (2001), *Postcard from Canberra* (2004), *There's Something About a Rose* (2012), *Ragged Edges* (2013) and *Music of the Heart* (2014). Her poem 'Conversation with trees after fire', published in *Postcard from Canberra* (2004), was in the exhibition City of Trees in 2013 and was recorded for the National Library's Oral Collection.

Jennie Fraine lives in Victoria, between two rivers; she learned about flood and fire growing up in the Barmah Forest. She discovered famine when teaching in Zambia in the 1970s. Her first collection of poetry, *The Cast Changes*, was runner-up in the Anne Elder Award. Jennie prefers to work as an Interactive Poet at festivals, writing poetry on the spot for as many people as possible on topics of interest to them. Her current passion is creating poetic maps with communities. She created *Mapping Moorabool in Poetry*, a freestanding map and booklet in 2013. She practises writing daily.

Hazel Hall is both a musicologist and café poet. Music wanders into her poetry habitually. She founded the ekphrastic group School of Music Poets in 2012. Hazel has published in journals, anthologies and chapbooks here and overseas, more recently *Eucalypt, Skylark, Sotto, Burley, Ragged Edges* and *The Melody Lingers On*. Her poem 'Kamikaze' was runner up for the 2012 Michael Thwaites award. With fellow poet John Collard, she recently launched the collection *Sugar Loaf and Humming Birds*. Hazel is currently working on *Memories of Sound*, a collection of poems based on her musical travels. She blogs at hazelhallpote.blogspot.com/

Helga Jermy migrated from the English Midlands to the north-west coast of Tasmania more than twenty years ago, where she is employed as a social worker. Her poems have been published recently in journals, anthologies and online including *Regime-Magazine of New Writing, Rabbit, Sotto, A Hundred Gourds* and *Australian Poetry* poems of the week. She is winner of Australian Poetry 'poem of the year 2013'. The poem 'Fire Storm' was written following the devastating bushfires in southeast Tasmania in January 2013.

Kathy Kituai is an award winning poet, diarist, founder and facilitator of the Limestone Tanka Poets. Since 1990, Kathy Kituai has facilitated workshops in SA, NSW, ACT and Scotland, receiving two Canberra Critics Circle awards. She has published three free verse poetry collections, three tanka collections (two with Amelia Fielden) including CD, three anthologies including *Ragged Edges* (2014), an NBC documentary for radio and a children's book. *Deep in the Valley of Teabowls* is forthcoming soon. Kathy has worked with dancers, visual artists, a musician, a potter and a photographer. She is published in Japan, UK, USA, Canada New Zealand, PNG and Australia.

Peter Kunz is a Canberra poet who has been writing since his childhood. Both a librarian and a researcher, he has worked at a number of Canberra cultural institutions including the National Gallery of Australia, National Library of Australia and the National Film and Sound Archive. He is currently occupied with contract librarianship. His main interests are poetry, history, soccer, motor vehicles, languages, philately and travel. Peter considers poetry as a way for an individual to understand and express the desires, hopes, vicissitudes and wonder of the human condition and man's relationship to others, animals and objects within the world which envelopes him.

Victoria McGrath lives in Yass, NSW. She has won a number of poetry awards and was shortlisted in 2013 for the prestigious Newcastle Poetry Prize. She has been published widely, including *The Canberra Times*, and journals such as *Cordite* and *Five Bells*. Victoria has had a number of poems published in anthologies, most recently *Australian Love Poems* 2013 (Inkerman and Blunt) and *Stars Like Sand, Australian Speculative Poetry* (IP) 2014. She's performed in a range of events including as featured poet at the Bundanoon Winterfest in 2011 and 2012. She is currently working on a manuscript titled *Hot*.

Fiona McIlroy majored in English Language & Literature (BA 1970 University of Melbourne), and then lived in pioneering rural cooperatives for twenty years, teaching in small schools and raising three children. Since moving to Canberra in 1992, Fiona has published a poetry collection *Taste of a Poem* (Ginninderra Press, 2009) and been published in several anthologies. Fiona won the Poetry Prize in the HRAFF competition 2010, and organises the Poetry in Motion train Canberra to Sydney on a biannual basis. She also facilitates a weekly poetry group at a Watson café as Café Poet in Residence with Australian Poetry.

Joe Massingham was born in the UK but has lived the second half of his life in Australia. Major employment has been as a Navy officer, university student from first degree to PhD, tutor, lecturer and Master of Wright College, University of New England, NSW. He has run his own writing and editing business but retired early because of cancer and heart problems and now spends time waiting to see medical practitioners, writing poetry and prose and smelling the roses. He has had work published in Australia, Canada, Eire, India, Nepal, New Zealand, UK, and USA.

Bob Morrow spent his childhood and youth in Sydney, worked and studied in south-east Asia and the United States for many years, and now lives in Melbourne. He fell into writing poetry while in Ireland searching for his great-grandfather's origins, and his poems, which have been widely published in Australian literary journals, often explore themes of family, belonging and a sense of place. His chapbook, *Moving On*, was released in 2013 by Mark Time Books of Castlemaine, Victoria. A keen body-surfer, Bob divides his time between Melbourne, the bush and a Bass Strait beach. morrow@bigpond.net.au.

Lizz Murphy, the Irish-Australian poet, was Highly Commended in the Blake Poetry Prize and a finalist in the Aesthetica Poetry Competition (UK) in 2013. Her awards include the 2011 Rosemary Dobson Poetry Prize (co-winner), a 2006 CAPO-Singapore Airlines Travel Award and the 1998 ACT Creative Arts Fellowship (Literature). She has published twelve books. Her seven poetry titles include *Portraits* and *Six Hundred Dollars* (PressPress), *Walk the Wildly* (Picaro), *Stop Your Cryin* (Island) and *Two Lips Went Shopping* (Spinifex: print & e-book). She hopes to publish another collection this year. Her poetry is widely published in Australia and overseas. Blog: lizzmurphypoet.blogspot.com

Moya Pacey: Ginninderra Press published Moya's first collection, *The Wardrobe* in 2009. It was runner-up for the ACT Writers' Centre Poetry Award. Her poetry is published widely in Australia and overseas and has won prizes. Most recently, one of her poems appeared on an ACTION bus in Canberra and several of her poems featured in the Canberra Centenary project 'City of Trees' installation at the National Library of Australia. She published a pamphlet of eighteen poems, *Always Me*, in December 2013 and is working towards a second collection.

Gregory Piko lives in Yass, New South Wales. Gregory was awarded joint first place in the 2013 W.B. Yeats Poetry Prize. His poetry has appeared in various journals and anthologies including *Page Seventeen*, *Famous Reporter*, *The Best Australian Poems 2012* (Black Inc, 2012), The Australian Poetry Members' Anthology: *Poems 2013* and *Haiku in English: The First Hundred Years* (W.W. Norton, 2013).

Sandra Renew writes poetry to express the purpose of poets in exploring the complexities and possibilities of the human condition and giving expression to the social conscience of the community. She has published poems in various chapbooks, including her own *Inventing Siberia*, fifteen poems from a journey on the Trans Siberian Railway, online in *Sotto* and in *Burley Journal*. In 2011 she was short listed for the ACT Writers' Michael Thwaites Award. Sandra's latest project, editing *In Response to Triage*, a chapbook of poems on Afghanistan in collaboration with artist Karen Bailey, was launched in February 2014.

Brenda Saunders is a Sydney poet and artist of Aboriginal and British descent. She has published three collections of poetry. Her most recent is *The Sound of Red* (Ginninderra Press, 2013). She has also been published in selected anthologies and poetry journals and is featured in *Best Australian Poems 2013* (Black Inc Publications). Brenda is a member of DiVerse Poets who read their ekphrastic poetry at Sydney art galleries. She has recently returned from a Resident Fellowship stay at CAMAC Arts Centre in France, where she worked translating her poetry into French.

John Karl Stokes is an Australian author and poet whose work has been published widely in Australia, Europe, Japan and the USA. He has won or been shortlisted for many major prizes, including the Blake, Newcastle and Rosemary Dobson Prizes for Poetry. He has represented Australia in overseas festivals. Publication credits include numerous journals, such as *Meanjin*, *Island*, *Ulitarra* and *Voices*, and the collections *A River in the Dark* (Five Islands Press), *Dancing in the yard at Eden* (Orta San Giulio, Italy), and his upcoming collection *Fire in the Afternoon* (Halstead Press) to be released in 2014.

Robyn Sykes, Australian Women's Bush Poetry Performance Champion, uses her poetry to bring to life the people and issues of rural Australia. After graduating from and working at Sydney University, Robyn moved with her BSc (Hons) to her husband's family farm near Binalong, where she spent the next thirty years writing, observing and learning. She raised four sons, edited the *Yass Tribune*, won the Bryan Kelleher Award and was an Australian Poetry Slam NSW finalist. Her 2013 collection, *Voices of the Fire*, was shortlisted for Published Poem, Single and Album of the Year in the 2014 Australian Bush Laureate Awards.

Maree Teychenné (pronounced Tay-shen-ay) has won state, national and international awards for her short stories, poetry, stage plays, song lyrics and film scripts. She's had many works published in the UK, Germany, US, New Zealand and Russia and performed on stage in Australia. Maree recently co-won the Children's Book Prize in the 2013 ACT Writing and Publishing Awards for her humorous literacy book, *My Aunt Ate a Plate*. Maree has a Music and Education degree from the University of Melbourne and writes full-time. Websites: www.trickywords.net.au and www.capaldoteychenne.com

Rod Usher is an Australian novelist and poet living in Extremadura, Spain. His third novel, *Poor Man's Wealth*, was published by HarperCollins in 2011. His third poetry collection, *Convent Mermaid*, is now available from Interactive Press, Brisbane.

Mira Walker: A cauldron of sources feeds Mira Walker's poetry. From her early life in Melbourne to her study of humanities and law at ANU and to time as a waiter, activist, unionist and welfare worker in Canberra. Her love of poetry has been nourished by local workshops and classes and appetised by reading, running, gardening and good food. She writes with and of love.

Adrienne White is a Canberra-based poet, currently studying at the Australian National University. She has a particular interest in Australian history.

Paul Williamson has published poems on eclectic topics in magazines including *Quadrant*, *Cordite*, *Burley*, *Five Bells*, *Eucalypt*, *Short and Twisted*, *Bukker Tillibul*, *This Next Wave*, *Hands like Mirrors*, *Tamba*, *Magic Cat* (UK), *Skylark* (UK), *Ribbons* (US) and *Gusts* (Canada). His poetry arrived after three research degrees (two in Science and one nominally in Arts but apparently in Sociology). He writes poems to clarify feelings and impressions, and then record them. His collections are *The DNA Bookshelf* and *Moments from Red Hill*, released in 2013.

Kathryn Yuen: After a lifetime as a mother of four, wife, and daughter, Kathryn Yuen is finally a poet, songwriter, playwright, screenwriter, theatre reviewer, storyteller and actress. She is currently filming *Maximum Choppage* with Matchbox pictures/ABC/NBC. She has been published in print and online including *WA Poets Poetry d'Amour*, *Otoliths*, *Clockwise Cat*, and *Papercuts*. Kathryn recently came second in the Peter Cowan National Patron's Poetry Prize. She has an upcoming monologue about loss and motherhood to be staged soon.

www.ingramcontent.com/pod-product-compliance
Lightning Source LLC
LaVergne TN
LVHW011737060526
838200LV00051B/3212